Dear Letters in the Red Box

Dear Letters in the Red Box

Poems by

Sarah Stern

© 2026 Sarah Stern. All rights reserved.
This material may not be reproduced in any form, published,
reprinted, recorded, performed, broadcast,
rewritten or redistributed without
the explicit permission of Sarah Stern.
All such actions are strictly prohibited by law.

Cover image by Henri Matisse (1869–1954), "The Red Studio."
1911. Oil on canvas, 71 1/4" x 7' 2 1/4" (181 × 219.1 cm).
MoMA, New York City. Provided by Public Domain Image
Library, Rayleigh, UK
Author photo by Claire Holt
www.claireholtphotography.com

ISBN: 978-1-63980-834-2
Library of Congress Control Number: 2025950192

Kelsay Books
502 South 1040 East, A-119
American Fork, Utah 84003
Kelsaybooks.com

For Michael, Willie, and Zoe

Also by Sarah Stern

Another Word for Love

But Today Is Different

We Have Been Lucky in the Midst of Misfortune

More Praise for Sarah Stern's Poetry

"Sarah Stern's poems combine praise and laments, odes and elegies, and compress complex feelings into love poems to the reader. She harnesses the 'strange muscle-beast' of the tongue into songs that taste like edible blossoms of joy and loss—more joy than sorrow. 'Absence has its own color,' Stern tells us—demonstrates—in magical, inventive lines. These lyrics teach us about letting go without drama. Sometimes poetry does the work of therapy; sometimes, the work of painting and song. It's all treasure, packed inside this volume, and now inside the reader's imagination."

—Marilyn Kallet, author of 18 books, including *How Our Bodies Learned* (Black Widow Press)

"Few writers develop the clarity of spirit, much less the skill, to let people and things dear to them arrive and reveal themselves. Sarah Stern, in her best poems, is such a writer. Breathtaking. And many of the poems in this collection are her best."

—Brooks Haxton, author of *They Lift Their Wings to Cry, Fading Hearts on the River, My Blue Piano*

"With her crystalline poetics, surprisingly clear-cut and full-throated at the same time, Sarah Stern offers her readers the piercing force of sage, tender, and impassioned utterance. Her artfully understated voice rouses us to grasp what it is to be human and to live vehemently and wholeheartedly. 'Sometimes a sentence / Makes you love a stranger,' Stern insightfully writes in words that propel us to experience this poet's formidable talents and compassion."

—Yerra Sugarman, author of *Forms of Gone, The Bag of Broken Glass,* Ph.D. in Creative Writing and Literature, University of Houston

"Sarah Stern has written an utterly frank, headlong, passionate, and deeply engendered book of a woman in mid-life. She writes out of her own longings, her devotions as a daughter and a mother, her fiery supplications. *But Today Is Different* may be printed with ink, but it was written with fire."

—Edward Hirsch, author of *A Poet's Glossary, The Living Fire: New and Selected Poems*

"Sarah Stern's first collection of poems, *But Today Is Different,* is a marvel. Wise, compassionate, erotic, plain-spoken, studded with wonderful moments—a black goat with blue eyes, an aging mother's clavicle 'like a Calder mobile,' an iconic lipstick stain on a coffee cup—Stern's vision puts a shine on the ordinary (a trip to Macy's, a scraped knee) and gives it back to us as something wondrous and new. A new voice, in which readers will hear echoes of Philip Levine and Grace Paley . . . and a real achievement."

—Cynthia Zarin, author of *The Ada Poems, An Enlarged Heart: A Personal History*

"In *Another Word for Love,* Sarah Stern searches for meaning in a broken world. She delights in things around her, whether the El in New York or trees in New Hampshire, finding in them keys to her inner life. I read this book in the light of her clarity, exactitude, and fine intelligence."

—Grace Schulman, author of *Without a Claim*

"Vivid and opaque, innocent and sophisticated, Sarah Stern's poems in *Another Word for Love* are so full of life, never more than when they hint at death, that they refuse to sit still on the page. It's us she's catching in these glimmering nets."

—Karen Durbin, *Elle*

"Sarah Stern is a poet to watch and relish."

—*Jewish Book World*

Acknowledgments

With much appreciation and affection for the One O'clock Poets. With love to family and friends who have encouraged me all these years. With special thanks to Katrinka Moore, Janet R. Kirchheimer, Jeffrey M. Eisenbrey, Marilyn Kallet, Brooks Haxton, Yerra Sugarman, Edward Hirsch, Cynthia Zarin, Grace Schulman, Amy Gottlieb, Cindy Hochman, Jeffrey Craig Miller, Andrew Nagorski, Charlie Varon, the late Karen Durbin, and the Bronx Council on the Arts. With further appreciation for the editorial team of Kelsay Books, and especially for Karen Kelsay.

With immeasurable love and gratitude to my husband, Michael, and children, Willie and Zoe, and daughter-in-law, Ariel Gleaner.

The author gratefully acknowledges the following publications in which these poems have appeared or are forthcoming, some in earlier versions:

Abandoned Mine: "Empty Nesters," "*Siempre*"
Amelia: "Currant Parties with Heddy," "Michelangelo's Hebrew Teacher," "Coming to America"
DASH Literary Journal: "Her Clip-Ons"
Clockhouse: "Soup"
East on Central: "At the Planetarium in Yonkers," "The Mall"
First Literary Review-East: "War"
Parks & Points: "Marconi Beach"
SLAB: "Under the Sugar Maple"
Slipstream: "Oil Paint"
The Ravens Perch: "After," "What It Was"
Treasure House: "The Cleaners"

Visions International: The World Journal of Illustrated Poetry:
    "The Narrows"
Wayfinding: Poetry celebrating America's parks and public lands:
    "Marconi Beach"
What Rough Beast (Indolent Books): "The Madmen"

Contents

Part I: What She Left Me

Soup	23
American Road Trip	25
Flesh	26
Haibun for Mom's Papers	27
Her Clip-Ons	28

Part II: Tea Party in a Foreign Land

High Heels	31
Poison Ivy	32
Dear Letters in the Red Box	33
The Cleaners	34
Currant Parties with Heddy	35
Greenland	37

Part III: It's Too Early to Write of These Times

Seeing Rilke, April 2020	41
The Rabbits	42
The Madmen	43
Animal Sijo	44
Palindrome	45
Reverie	46
Pale Blue	47

Part IV: Small Birds

The Chairs	51
Spuyten Duyvil	52
Moderna on the Last Day of Passover and Easter Sunday	53
Venice	54
Ruby's	55
Siempre	56
Calluses	57
Bianca	58

Part V: Dancing in the Storm

Worms	61
Jupiter	62
The Narrows	63
Michelangelo's Hebrew Teacher	64
The Passover Story	65
I've tried to write a poem many times	66
Marconi Beach	67

Part VI: How Beautiful We Really Were

Good	71
Coming to America	72
Paula,	73
Mackerel	74
For the Young Men Who Threw Away My Astroglide at the Airport	75

Counting   76
Art   77

Part VII: Her Skinself

After   81
Mom Again   82
What It Was   84
4215   85
Brooklyn   86
Oil Paint   87

Part VIII: Travel Notes

Under the Sugar Maple   91
Colorado Corridor Trails   92
The Mall   94
War   95
At the Planetarium in Yonkers   96
Golden Pothos   97
Chanukah   98
Empty Nesters   99

Part I:

What She Left Me

Soup

She hung laundry in the backyard
the way she did many things—
there was sadness in the inquiry—
but also a fiery freedom, like yes,
we're still here, you bastards.

And the bastards were any number
of beings across time. The bras
and sweatpants, her flowered dresses,
her husband's work shirts, the socks she darned.

All the pieces in the sun
somehow brought the sea and shells
and what we started to remember.

*

I can tell by the way he enjoys
his soup with his shirt off
that this is a man who stops at
nothing for pleasure.

I'm across the street on the opposite fire escape
thinking about pleasure—how we're all vessels
porcelain bowls, ornate, sweet and savory.

The traffic below, humming along
on the avenue. The soup, the shirt,
the vertical light across the afternoon.

*

The first thing he says to the cow each morning is
"Hi, honey, how was your evening?"
Trudy looks back at him, lifting her head.
Her face is black with a wide white blaze
that drops down her nose,
reminding him that he is a small creature.

*

How do we let our bodies dance?
Like this, she said.
We don't let anything—it happens—
the swing of it, in the middle.
I wish I could let go, not realize I'm moving,
like water, it knows nothing of itself.
Shadow too, across the stairs, it knows nothing
of its long lines that move ahead of us.

American Road Trip

Too much of something is never good, but that's always what we want, isn't it? Especially with the road stretched out in front of us. We want to keep going. See it all. Touch it all. Fill up with so much love we burst with the new season's buds. But all of this can't be. We don't have enough time. Just praise. How good it is.

Three beautiful girls stand in a row on the 6 train looking at their cell phones in unison—their bodies touching—a continuum of innocence. I don't know if it's really true about innocence, but I do appreciate their teen profiles, their concentrated loveliness, and the motion of the rest of us in our seats moving north with them.

Did anyone ever really care about us? We thought someone did, maybe someone we didn't know yet, but knew us, caught us in a frame as we turned the corner in the neighborhood where we used to watch things happen. Like when the ice-cream truck pulled up on our street and when the couple that lived across the way finally called it quits. He packed up his car one morning and she stood in the front yard alone, finally.

Suppose we could move quietly the way a moose moves her body through the twilight. She was twenty feet from the path—her head low and still—taking in the falling light around us. As if we had been placed there by something we still can't name. How large and silent she is, even now, so many years later.

Flesh

The moon sliver last night
Reminded me of nothing but winter
Each season we are bears
But our hides are no match
So we layer thick
Howling like wolves.
We're really
Not an orange
With its peel, but a plum
A purple plum in summer
Easily marred.
My heart is a moon plum.
Henry Hudson Parkway
The dark trees
Fly by in our car
Catching us in mid-sentence
The sleet makes its own noise
Against the windshield
We listen
The wonder of its flesh
Small fire for a new year.

Haibun for Mom's Papers

Over a year of reading them, taking notes. Now I go through my own. Perhaps the arc of a life is just that, and Mother is Mother in her love, rage, disappointments, and pride. I'm interested in how I respond to her writings, but I can't know yet. I have to wait and see what her tomatoes and arugula do to me. "The Osage Orange Tree," "The Green Man," "Mrs. Adlerbloom," "Oma's Time"— her poems dissolve me like sugar in water. Her bluntness struck me as a child, but now I can name it. I think what she wanted most was to be in the world without impediment. *To see the light fall through the forest.* To be. To swim, yes, eight laps. Her Chaim, *a dream.*

I love you, Mommy
I see you in the garden
Still a mystery.

Her Clip-Ons

Wind through pines. Swwwooosh.
First sounds and sights you never forget.
Or farmer's cheese. Mom loved it, and I remembered that years
later at Stop & Shop. She would spread it
on bread and enjoy it with coffee. Still in a rectangular package.
When she told me she didn't want to live anymore,
I said, *how about for me?*
She said she'd had enough.
There was nothing left of her except the flat light
that came through the old house windows.
I keep thinking about *enough,*
the deep me somewhere
and how things take on their own lightness.
I wake up with what she left me.
Her deep. Her clip-on earrings I turned to posts.
They go through me now.

Part II:

Tea Party in a Foreign Land

High Heels

High heels and a drink always intrigued her. It's not something she grew up with, but, yes, she remembered that her mom had bought her a first pair of lilac pumps. At seventeen she felt invincible. Holding a daiquiri and speaking to people. That was a discovery. The awkwardness gone—at least for a time. So many years later, she realizes she's a private person and that may be a good thing.

*

She remembered going upstairs to the room where her mom kept the papers and more in that box. Her mom took everything out, one at a time. The passports, the receipts, the 1946 love letters written at the New York Public Library, the Western Union telegram: *Arrived in Paris.* The photos in no order. The house, grandparents, all the kids, Cousin Heddy, the station wagon. Mom would close the box and put it back in the closet for next time. It was a routine that neither understood, but they took satisfaction in its containment like a short day in winter.

Poison Ivy

We read the same book and you
love how it starts and I,
how it ends. Or tea and biscuits.
Or the cat. Even poison ivy.

Do you think we could ever
share the same thing—
experience the identical feeling?
I don't think so.

Sprouting its three seductive leaves
at each auburn juncture. Beauty.
Blisters ooze and itch.
But we agree on this: we shouldn't touch it,

which makes me think about museums.
No touching, stand back.
Those trios on the trail
a strange connection,

art and the venomous vine
that my mother taught me to recognize
early on. If it brushed against you,
you'd have to wash everything you were wearing

hang them out on the clothesline,
later, fold and layer them
in the wicker basket.
They were stiff and smelled of summer.

Dear Letters in the Red Box

What do I do with you, thin and fading? Their marriage, September 1946. Soon after, Dad off to the Sorbonne for medical school, Mom joining him that December.

Dad's Paris:

> "The leaves outside my windows are the colors of autumn. It makes my heart feel sad and glad at the same time, *shatzele*. I love you so much it hurts."

or this,

> "I love you like Uncle Karl loved Jenny."

or this,

> "Today there wasn't a ray of sunshine—Parisian winter weather. Oh yes, there was when I looked at your photo, comrade. You light up my room."

> "I am well, eat like a professional wrestler, sleep like a newborn babe, but am terribly lonesome for you."

> "I gave my first intravenous injection."

Maybe snippets are never enough.

> "I saw you there so clearly."

Always.

The Cleaners

The man who counted
my father's shirts
had numbers up
his forearm. Ironed,
the shirts hung side
by side above him.

The six black digits
came back to me
in dreams, where I
ran from the men who
shaved my grandfather's head.

The laundryman's
English was heavy.
O's stayed in his mouth longer.
His belly
sat over his belt.

A raisin Danish was always
on the counter.
He liked sweetness
on his thumb and forefinger.
He handed me the ticket.

Currant Parties with Heddy

Heddy slapped horses and children.
Fear spread across her face
only during lightning.
But when she entered her garden,
gentleness.

Her large hands
plucked the currants
from their twisted stems.
She let them roll from her palm
into a tin bucket.

Speaking the Black Forest dialect,
she worked on her knees,
my mother beside her.
I felt strangely included
in those talks.

The words were incomprehensible
but familiar.
The language lulled me.
I was at a tea party
in a foreign land.

After the ripe ones were gathered
Heddy rose methodically,
bending from the waist,
letting her arms hang,
stretching her strong back,

until the blood rushed to her face,
and she straightened
to meet my gaze.
She was smiling
with the bucket full.

Greenland

I see my life
on the screen
as the plane soars.
Can I live in Greenland?
I love you, Negev yellow daisy,
Tanacetum santolinoides, connate petals.

Eilat crescent.
Across the Red Sea, Jordan,
lights flicker.
Moon palms sway
in their lizard-like way.

After trips
I'd always call my parents.
I'm home.
That made it so.
I say it out loud now.

Part III:

It's Too Early to Write of These Times

Seeing Rilke, April 2020

You must change your life.
I read that line in the paper
The trees swaying, immutable today
Light careens through them
I'm looking for order
Cardinal, catbird, chickadee
Blue jay, red-tailed hawk
They sing of things we can't know yet

This is the spring of birds
We hear them now on our terraces
No United, American, Delta
Fierce and feral, the forsythias fire-yellow
The magnolias open
I dare you, they say.

The Rabbits

Someone was blowing a shofar
on the street corner this afternoon.
On my bike, it caught me mid-pedal.
I thought of my father and his fasting.

It's too early to write of these times.
Bees maneuver in the cucumber blossoms,
accommodating and yellow,
pollen and patience.

The storm felled the trees,
revealing the rot that runs
through—winds roar
and we are exposed.

Five rabbits
in the back of our building.
Momma and her babies munching away.
I want to get down and be small with them.

They chew on. I get too close and they scatter
I can't get enough of their big feet—
and those eyes—looking at me in this plague.
Their noses twitching.

The Madmen

There's always another part of the story.
The cardinal's red by the bird feeder
just before the starlings scatter.
The small snowdrifts mounting
the trees. My parents' French.

My own bold
declarations before the crowd of madmen.
It happened last night between or in a dream.
I stood in a long dress,
took a deep breath, and started to speak

about the story we don't know.
The madmen knocked on the ground
with their sticks. I waited until they stopped.
And started to speak again,
full-throated. They began beating on the ground again.

I waited, started once more. Strange words
came out of me. The madmen were still,
almost for the first time.
The air nestled in on itself.
I stretched my arms out and evaporated.

Shimmering in water light,
I woke up fully flesh again—
a fish of sorts, new fins and scales,
a tail too, red mouth—
all me in this early hour.

Animal Sijo

We turned the bend and all three of us let out a howl.
We were the same animal with fur and wings.
It was an Agnes Martin sky, hints of color

we couldn't name. We kept turning in the Guggenheim
in those years of what I now think of as *before the storm,*
her painting, the one we looked back on before we left.

Palindrome

I didn't choose to stand next to you.
My body brought me there.
I rode to you on a current
of what do we call it? I don't know.
But there we were next to each other
in the crowd and the people
listening to us whisper about
the food and wine we wished
we had brought with us.
All of it appeared somehow and we
shared it with everyone in our midst.
I can't explain the joy.

I can't explain the joy.
It appeared somehow
and we shared it with everyone in our midst.
There we were next to each other
in the crowd and the people
listening to us whisper about
the food and wine we wished
we had brought with us.
I rode to you on a current
of what do we call it? I don't know.
My body brought me there.
I didn't choose to stand next to you.

Reverie

To cross the log
we had to hold on to each other.
It was hard to keep our balance.

We weren't running from anything
but our own fears.
And then—there it was—

firm ground and the sound of a dog, invisible to us,
barking, but we knew she saw
something in the high tree, first reckoning.

Pale Blue

I can't go through all my mother's papers
but I have to

Her German passport with the large
J on it
Her eyes—pale blue
The gray trees of winter and that silver blue before sunset

She's in the blue diminishing
The horror of J rides through me

She loved geology
And me, a little girl

Somewhere out there
Fading in the sound of her voice.

Part IV:

Small Birds

The Chairs

No one knew when the snow had started.
Some thought the early-morning hours
with the owls and coyotes.

Soft and thin like lace, it covered the chairs
in all the yards for miles and miles.
Snow made the color of things pop open—

the blues reflected back at us, a lake
we dove into. The trees, their trunks gray
whales, call in the slow wind, reminding me

of the winters we were together,
when we'd rush outside in the season's first,
not knowing, how could we, how could we—

Spuyten Duyvil

Walking up the steps from the train,
I see a dead yellow-shafted Northern Flicker
must have hit a window of The Henry, new building
under the bridge. Look at its red nape, black whisker, yellow

streaks on its flight and tail feathers.
I keep staring. He stays with me.
The peaceful transfer of power.
My father would speak of it. He marveled.

What I know is the number of stairs to the top.
That naming things is good. That as long as we can count, there is
an accounting. The paper outlines a particular disaster with such
precision, timelines, charts that echo the era.

Dear Reader, we must try harder.
The common bumper sticker COEXIST
on a yellow Volkswagen, dented and dated,
catches me on the old avenue.

Moderna on the Last Day of Passover and Easter Sunday

Benedicta gave me the second dose
at the Bronx High School of Science.

She asked my name and birthdate twice.
And then I asked hers. Blessing.

Venice

I will remember how these days
overlapped into weeks,
months gathering until the new year.

Love and loss.
To write of them is really a luxury,
I didn't know it then.

Look for the lines that soothe.
To live in a strange factory of trees and words.
A couple asleep in a gondola,

leaning into each other,
their mouths open in Venice.
It's supposed to be funny.

How vulgar in these years of plenty,
and not plenty.
My life too.

Guilt, grudges, ugliness.
The turning inward.
My dark heart, I hear you.

Ruby's

Her window looks out at the bar
that swells and shrinks with the seasons.
Winter, especially around the holidays, brings
hordes. Sometimes there's a line
around the block. Summer, when the city empties,
the place does too. She likes it best in summer.

From her perch she can make out the patrons,
their movements, even their drinks. Knows the
regulars like the back of her hand.
She goes in there sometimes
to remember who she used to be
in the old neighborhood.

Siempre

Siempre, that's what the man at the corner
would say when he'd begin a soliloquy about his life.
Each day we heard a different version
of what I imagine were
his war memories intertwined
with the now we were all in.
But, *Siempre, Siempre* seemed to be his anchor
for something significant
that I wanted to know more about.
I connected it to his hands that moved
in the air, small flitting birds.
This happened in Spain one summer
when I thought there was an order to things.

Calluses

My grandfather had thick calluses
on his hands. My mother
was always delighted when she shook

someone's hand and they too had them,
as if that person, whoever they were,
brought Julius back to her

after his travels in the Black Forest
when he'd dismount his horse and
lift her up, suspending her even now.

Bianca

Sasha found a kitty in his beard one morning—
he woke up to a soft purr and thought
his blanket had become a living thing, but, no, the night
left him Bianca, the name just came out of him,
from where he didn't know, her green eyes sparkled
with such intensity that Sasha thought he was still dreaming
but, no, Sasha was awake and alive,
Bianca hungry.

Part V:

Dancing in the Storm

Worms

The afternoon comes in on itself
all bright desire to love you
like we used to before the fall,
before the unraveling.
The nests remain in winter trees,
stay put in this mad weather,
the intimate weaving, the busyness.
The silver strands from somewhere else flicker in the sun,
wound tight in the old beds.
The birds recycle without crusade or fanfare.
They know it already, desperately.
I want to live inside their abandoned places,
wait for the worms,
your beak in mine.

Jupiter

He's looking for Jupiter's moons on Johnson Avenue.
People gather around, but we can't
see anything, clouds in the way.

It doesn't matter. I take it as a good sign—that someone
hauls out a telescope and welcomes strangers.
Jupiter has 79 moons, 26 still unnamed.

Can we name them for the dead?
The dead who wouldn't recognize these places any longer.
The new wizards on the sidewalk who nod now.

Sometimes the world is so fragile I want to cradle it
like a newborn. How she
peeks through

the strange wind of this cold spring.
The genius, the bright lights.
How the leaves fracture in the western Bronx.

I hear a voice from the back of the crowd.
*Hey, weren't you the guy in Great Barrington
last summer looking for stars out on the field?*

No, it wasn't me. That was someone else, he mumbles.
We're all trying to name things
in the dark,

reconfigure what was and what will be,
the marble moons,
their exquisite colors we fly into all night.

The Narrows

It was winter 1987 and snowing
        There was a party at NYU
I slept over at Janet's dorm

I remember dancing, large windows
        Walking tonight through Washington Square Park I look up
For some sign of redemption

I search in these warm months
        When the nakedness of what is shoots by us like stars
In the heavy wave of trees, fountains, and flesh

I want this to be a long poem
        Winding through the years
Like the stories that begin *Once upon a time*

Once upon a time there was a little girl
        Who liked to catch things in streams
Tadpoles, minnows, and newts

The light flooded in too, the way it did this summer
        How it ricocheted off the sandstone canyons
The rappelers made their way down, carrying their gear

There was satisfaction in seeing them touch ground
        I'm lost in this new season
I come back to dancing in the storm.

Michelangelo's Hebrew Teacher

Far down the hall I see David's
whole stone body fit into my camera's
frame. Closer, I take in parts—
toes, hands, back, chest.

My fourth-grade teacher, Rabbi Citron,
had long fingers. When he pushed chalk
along the blackboard, writing from right to left,
his veins rode up on his forearm

like horses' reins and made me
love him secretly in my notebook.
In the gallery the circle
of lights glide over David,

as angels do, making a segment glow
and another fall in shadow. In the dim
classroom Rabbi Citron looked over
our heads, through the window,

as though he needed more space
for his thoughts that filled
the room, leaving us feeling that
we also could lose ourselves in thought.

The Passover Story

Elijah comes late at night to my parents'
house, putting his old lips to the edge
of the silver cup my grandfather won
when he fought for the Germans in World War I.

The cup has tiny trophies molded
to its sides. Each year it comes out
of the cabinet. "Your grandfather Julius
was a good fighter," my mother says.

Looking at his photograph, his shaven head,
I try to imagine. I think of Julius and Klara.
He is the cup. Firm, ornate, filled with wine.
She's the crystal bowl

that comes out too this time of year.
The top comes off easily like a hat.
It catches light when it's empty. Tonight
she's filled with salt and sits by a glass of water.

I've tried to write a poem many times

about empty plastic bags stuck in trees.
I can't decide whether they are signs
of things that are lost or could have been
or even me and my younger selves.
I saw a movie once where the lens
focused on one in a honey locust.
The plastic swaying, iridescent,
beautiful on the big screen.

Marconi Beach

Midnight moon so bright
it made night
the negative of night.

Waves, late August,
foaming, the same mistakes
over and over

until what's left
is the flatness of things:
this black stone worn down,

the beach grasses too,
the horizontal lovers
beyond the break.

Part VI:

How Beautiful We Really Were

Good

No one would know
They were once lovers

Old friends now who've come together
For a meal on a Sunday in January

There was a rhythm to their outpourings
Like a stream that meanders through the forest

They hadn't seen each other in years
The food was good like they were

Bread and butter, barley soup,
A salad with beets and ricotta

Ending in an apple tart with coffee
Dinner was done

But she kept thinking about it
And how she was happy now.

She couldn't have imagined it years ago,
but, there it was, staring at her

like the fork and knife resting on her plate
and the vase of winter flowers at their table.

Coming to America

Apples stand seven feet high
at the Fairway Market, towering
over pears, tangelos, apricots.
Leek, romaine, Swiss chard make a green lane.
Cracked wheat, sourdough, Irish
soda bread. Magic. Anything is possible.

I think of Mother coming
to America where there was so much
even the bugs were fat.
And Lena from Odessa
who told me of her first supermarket visit
where she grew dizzy from the choices.

Outside, an old man plays
the violin, open case beside him.
I bring him in, nobody watches.
He dances on Granny Smiths, none fall.
He's young again. He jumps to the floor,
stuffs a fig wheel into his coat, and walks out.

Paula,

do you remember when we went
to the bowling alley that once stood
near Broadway and 231st Street?
We were in high school and
everything felt like we were rising.
We tried not to get knocked down.
When we did, we'd get up
with our fresh bodies, glowing,
unaware of how beautiful we really were.

Mackerel

The fish circled the diver who tried
to stay in the middle of the whirring

that moved with his thoughts as though the fish,
the water, the leaked light, he, himself, were all one—

a melding that he had never experienced
until then, or since. A revelation

that years later would come back to him
only in parts—sometimes the mass of mackerel

or the salt on his lips, or the floating in wizard blue.
Then he'd wake up, gasping for air, back on land.

For the Young Men Who Threw Away
My Astroglide at the Airport

I'm learning how to pack light
One carry-on, one knapsack
Last-minute thinking—
There's this, love, come what may, right?
Shoes off, belts too, electronics in the gray tubs
Hands up for the scanner.

They flag my blue carry-on
Pop it open, pull out the culprit, and say that the only way
I can board is to check the bag and go through security again—
Sure, go ahead, throw it out.

We make our way to the gates
On moving sidewalks, with passengers already delayed and angry,
Who have no idea of our nearly thirty years together.
It's all extraordinary—
The captains and stewards
Gleaming parked planes with their insignias
The bright morning in Newark—
Flying.

Counting

Mom said once,
It was all worth it because of you.

What did she mean?
I didn't want to know then

because *it* was too big, like a tarp
over everything. A house of worship.

But now I want to know.
When the temperature drops

Leaves burn at their edges
before they fall,

a fable of counting.
We can see Henry Hudson again.

The vista opens
and the doves shudder.

Art

We believe we met in our first
decade when we were learning
how the world worked, like lining up
in size order, how we could
draw what we wanted in class,
even paint on the easels and wear smocks.
We met painting something red.

Part VII:

Her Skinself

After

The just-finished rain made everything blunt
Tulips askew, breaking light

Reminding me
when my mother died that summer

And I needed to see her body
One last time

Her skinself
The grass and fire hydrants.

Mom Again

The goldfish in the park are preoccupied in their orangeness.
The couple on the 1 train riding north holding bags of apples.

*

At the Anne Carson reading I hear:
> *As if the flaps of time were folded wrong*
> *This is a room waiting for nothing*
> *The silence between two thoughts*
> *The blue comes up through many grays*
> *Why paint? Because people keep paintings*
> *Stillness takes time*
> *I like to keep the hesitation*
> *I'm an in-between thing*
> *People stitch their lips shut as a form of protest*
> *Mewing.*

*

The body shifting. Moon menopause. Hot head. Was yours?
Did everything go day-glo for you?
Did the colors of things become the things themselves?

*

I want to meet you now, years gone already, tell you things. I wouldn't know where to start. *So busy,* you'd say. I had no idea, when you died, how much you'd still be there with me, lurking. Yes, is that you in the mirror? But that's the least of it.

What It Was

Riding away from you,
I eat the whole apple—
flesh, core, pits.

You are light and shadow,
everything and nothing.
You have left a sapling

that has already taken root
below stone, making room for me.
A wellspring was always there.

We break together, forming
something that escapes
through our nostrils.

The hairs in our noses
singed from what it was.

4215

The numbers I press twice to enter the Sheepshead Bay
memory unit where she lives now,
my teacher, my beautiful friend—
pictures of her mom we return to over and over,
from the animal books, the big cats roar back at us,
her new words come out in the jumbled fur-fin kingdom,
when we recognize one
we repeat it and laugh,
pick out shoes for the walk
along the water to our window seats at the café
where we order what we want,
Diet Coke, Turkish coffee, shrimp, eggs, fries, and chocolate cake.
Toddlers eat at other tables,
gurgling about things we can't know,
and the great gulls play outside
swooping for us, high and wide.

Brooklyn

The trees and more
trees in the deep yonder.
It helps her to remember
the clear water, blue water
that flowed at the bottom
of the valley like some dream
we almost had.
Demented and gracious, she
stares at me. I reach out.
We hold each other in the dark woods.

Oil Paint

> *There are all sorts of things in my head*
> *but it's so late now.*
> —Georgia O'Keeffe

When we arrive she is sleeping
Then wakes and we walk to the living room
Where she sits and laughs, whispering things

A piano tuner
With an assistant and an attaché case
keeps hitting A, then A-sharp

The keys mark time
In the memory unit with the bay out there
All sorts of things in my head

Georgia too—
When moving toward oil paint
A, then A-sharp

She falls asleep again
All sorts of things in my head
Our bodies, it's late now.

Part VIII:

Travel Notes

Under the Sugar Maple

I remember how much I love you
here—it's always from a distance—
with the grass, the cardinal,
the small child bent almost in half
the way the little ones can,
looking intently at things
that move below us.
And you're no longer here.

You're just beyond the hill,
where you hover like a new bee
this time of year, counting
the beamy leaves as they widen
in our midst, making everything buzz
open, blushing too.

Colorado Corridor Trails

We hike from lake to lake
Nymph, Dream, Emerald, Haiyaha.
Each a different shade of blue, almost green.
The speckled trout swim near.

Who makes such beauty?
At 9,000 feet, I'm lightheaded, headachy,
as though my brain has tilted in its casing.
I think of separations

that sculpted the Rockies by glacial episodes,
and here we are with our water bottles,
our daughter far ahead
in this light that streams down like manna.

The four elk already lying on the high grass
preparing for the night
watching us as though we were some tiny stars
that fell just then for them.

My body no longer mine
in the bevy of aspen trees,
dark eyes on their green bark.
They stare at us.

Maybe it was the thin air,
or the rainbow on the fish, or
the large pupils running
along the tree flanks,

but I said out loud
I'm sorry.
The elk raised their heads and
we turned down the mountain.

The Mall

Sometimes the broccoli at the market is enough
        or the way the light falls right through
the trees—a perfect line
        that startles you, then it shifts.

In DC last weekend there was a sign
        on the Mall that said everything is temporary.
I took comfort in it. The carousel too.
        I walked closer and saw the painted horses

and the mirrors that reflected us.
        I wanted to recite everything that I know
while I rode a horse, but instead
        I bought a pretzel.

I sat on a bench with my mustard and salt,
        watching the children circling,
their parents waving,
        shouting at them to hold tight.

War

Four unmatched shoes
Strewn on cracked cobblestones.
We look at photos.

At the Planetarium in Yonkers

We sat back in darkness and heard
that in millions of years our galaxy
will crash with another. No one will
get hurt, but the stars will shift and
new constellations will appear.

The little boys behind us
were kicking our seats, as they
wanted to move on with the afternoon—
to run in the wet grass.
Mommy, pleeeze, we heard them say.

I was stuck on what a new Orion would look like.
I made a promise, then and there,
to let myself love everything that I could
the night sky, the boys behind us, you, my strangeness,
the wet grass, everyone who ever said *yes.*

Golden Pothos

I've had this vine since the '80s—
    What it knows about me.
        Lately, I don't recognize myself in my

Back and forth, my lily and tiger.
    Trimming away at the dead-end
        Growth this morning,

We make way for the quiet.
    Then the water and that sun that blasts
        over both of us from out yonder.

We almost quiver together
    With our unrelenting desire
        For something new and good, that tilt

Toward the truth.
    I think I believe that evil is stronger,
But good never gives up.

Chanukah

Dad would cut the large Shabbat candles in half
so that they'd fit nicely in the large silver
menorahs he'd bring down from the shelves,
about six going each night,
he'd set them in front of the windows.
Dad had a thing about light.
Mom always told him, *Enough*.

How could I know then
that all of it would become
a vision of what was:
my father's white flames
everywhere, roaring right
behind the glass.

Empty Nesters

When I stop and think of my parents
        adjusting their bicycles on the car
as they head west, there's a tenderness
        in the exploration.

Mom wrote travel notes on the back
        of a Tucson gas station flyer advertising
oil changes and more. Her observations: *Hot.*
        Almost lost the bikes. One tent pole
missing, but we made do.

Her night sky. Cassiopeia. Rock
        formations. Dad's additions:
Spoke to English tourists today. Lots of them.
        I see my parents tighten the bike-rack straps.
They get back in the car and pull away.

About the Author

Sarah Stern is the author of three poetry books: *We Have Been Lucky in the Midst of Misfortune* (Kelsay Books, 2018), *But Today Is Different* (Wipf and Stock Publishers, 2014), and *Another Word For Love* (Finishing Line Press, 2011). She is a six-time winner of the Bronx Council on the Arts BRIO Poetry Award, a recipient of two Pushcart Prize nominations, and several Poets & Writers Readings & Workshops Grants.

Stern is an educator at Poets House. She's taught poetry workshops at Poets House, WritingWorkshops.com, Off Campus Writers' Workshop (OCWW), the Marlene Meyerson JCC Manhattan, the New York Public Library, CSAIR Adult Learning Institute, Hostos Community College, the Bronx Zoo, Edgar Allan Poe Visitor Center, and privately. Stern is the founder of SDGS Solutions, a communications and marketing consultancy. She's worked at universities, cultural centers, and think tanks. She graduated from Barnard College and Columbia University's Graduate School of Journalism.

Learn more:
sarahstern.me

www.ingramcontent.com/pod-product-compliance
Lightning Source LLC
Chambersburg PA
CBHW022016160426
43197CB00007B/455